WHAT I FEEL

I AM LONELY

Beth Gottlieb

Gareth Stevens PUBLISHING

first concepts

I am lonely.
This means I feel alone.

Max is new in class.
He is lonely.

Max plays with
new friends.
He is not lonely.

Anna’s mom is at work.
She is lonely.

Sam's dad
comes home.
She hugs him.
She is not lonely.

Luke is sick today.
He misses school.
He is lonely.

Cam misses his friends.
Cam calls Dee.
He is not lonely.

chat.
Hello
Hi Everybody
Type Message Here...

Kim's mom takes a trip.
Kim misses her.
She is lonely.

Emma is lonely.
She plays with
her brother.
She feels better.

Everyone feels
lonely sometimes.
It's OK!

What makes you feel lonely?

Please visit our website, www.garethstevens.com. For a free color catalog of all our high-quality books, call toll free 1-800-542-2595 or fax 1-877-542-2596.

Library of Congress Cataloging-in-Publication Data

Names: Gottlieb, Beth author
Title: I am lonely / Beth Gottlieb.
Description: Buffalo, New York : Gareth Stevens Publishing, [2027] | Series: What I feel
Identifiers: LCCN 2025027203 (print) | LCCN 2025027204 (ebook) | ISBN 9781482476187 (library binding) | ISBN 9781482476170 (paperback) | ISBN 9781482476194 (ebook)
Subjects: LCSH: Loneliness in children–Juvenile literature | Loneliness–Juvenile literature | Emotions in children–Juvenile literature
Classification: LCC BF723.L64 G68 2027 (print) | LCC BF723.L64 (ebook) | DDC 152.4–dc23/eng/20250807
LC record available at https://lccn.loc.gov/2025027203
LC ebook record available at https://lccn.loc.gov/2025027204

Published in 2027 by
Gareth Stevens Publishing
2544 Clinton Street
Buffalo, NY 14224

Designer: Deanna Lepovich
Editor: Therese Shea

Photo credits: Cover Tartila/Shutterstock.com; cover, pp. 3, 5, 7, 9, 11, 13, 15, 17, 19, 21, 23 (texture) v_kulieva/Shutterstock.com; p. 3 Ann in the uk/Shutterstock.com; p. 5 Pressmaster/Shutterstock.com; p. 7 PeopleImages/Shutterstock.com; p. 9 Standret/Shutterstock.com; pp. 11, 21 fizkes/Shutterstock.com; p. 13 SofikoS/Shutterstock.com; p. 15 vectorfusionart/Shutterstock.com; p. 17 Ekaterina Ru/Shutterstock.com; p. 19 Ruslan Huzau/Shutterstock.com; p. 23 Christin Lola/Shutterstock.com.

Printed in China

CPSIA compliance information: Batch #QSGS27: For further information contact Gareth Stevens at 1-800-542-2595.